IT WORKS WORKBOOK

The Famous Little Red Book that
Makes your Dream come true

THIRD EDITION

SUCCESS BOOKS

This book is dedicated to you and the souls seeking to improve their condition in life.

You have within you a mighty power, anxious and willing to serve you

— RH JARRETT

CONTENT

If you KNOW
what you WANT
You can HAVE it

It Works | Workbook

Introduction

Do not wonder if this *It Works Workbook* can work for you. It can. All it requires is a little time and effort on your part. This workbook is intended to guide you page by page.

Based on the original version of *It Works, this workbook* will enhance your understanding of *It Works* and help you actualize your desires faster.

We wish you well in your journey of acquiring desirable possessions.

Rules:
- Do not skip the sections
- Do not skip the questions
- Do not pick it up and put it aside.

You will need:
- It Works by RH Jarrett
- A pencil
- An earnest desire to complete the workbook.

It Works | Workbook

DESIRE

All that spirits desire, spirits attain

KHALIL GIBRAN

Desire

To change your condition and manifest desirable possessions, you have to know and understand the difference between *merely wishing* and *earnest desire*.

There are many definitions of desire, but on this subject, we are most concerned about the desire for manifestation. We call it **earnest desire**.

Wish

A wish, in simple terms, means something to hope for. Hope is an expectation that something good might happen. Mere wishes are wants without a driving force (fuel). In essence, they lack potency that leads to nowhere but non-achievement.

No matter how good a car is, you can't drive a great distance without adequate fuel. It's the same way with merely wishing. Regardless of your object of desire, simply desiring it will not bring about its manifestation. It lacks the potency for actualization.

Name one thing in your life that you wanted but underneath was merely a wish?

Earnest Desire

To desire means to earnestly want something, a strong need to demand or claim a thing. *Earnest desire* is the opposite of *merely wishing*. It has a driving force. Its potency is based on the degree of intensity of the object desired. The stronger the desire, the stronger the force. It's this force that leads to potential actualization.

A thirsty desert traveler will leave all his other desires to find water to drink. As long as he is thirsty, his only thought will be drinking water. The driving force is the desire for water. His mind has been encapsulated with the thought of drinking water. This is his true desire, hence **earnest desire**.

(Object of desire + Intensity of thought)

Earnest Desire

Name one thing in your life that you earnestly desired that came into manifestation.

After reading IT WORKS, answer the following questions below as best as you can. If you find it difficult answering some of the questions, go back and reread the book or the chapter. It's important that you have a full understanding of the key concepts.

What is the real secret of obtaining desirable possessions?

"If wishes were horses, beggars would ride". What does that quote mean to you?

What is the cause of the difference in conditions in which men live?

It Works | Workbook

MIND

You are today where your thoughts have brought you; you will be tomorrow where your thoughts take you

JAMES ALLEN

Mind

The doctrine of dualism states that they are two kinds of reality. The physical (material world) and the spiritual (immaterial world) reality.

In the philosophy of mind, man has two minds: the outer (physical) and the inner (spiritual) mind.

These two minds are called the objective (physical) and the subjective (spiritual) mind. They are endowed with distinct attributes and power and capable of independent action to some extent.

What are the two kinds of mind?

Objective Mind

The objective mind is conscious (awake) of the physical world. It observes the world through the five physical senses. It guides man in the physical world, and its highest function is reasoning.

In less than 10 words, define the Objective mind?

What does the Objective mind mean to you?

How does the Objective mind affect your desire?

Subjective Mind

The subjective mind is conscious (aware) of the spiritual world. It is omnipotent. It has unlimited power and is capable of accomplishing anything. It perceives by intuition, serves as the seat of emotion and the repository of memory. It performs its highest function when the objective mind is in a suspended state.

In less than 10 words, define the Subjective mind?

What does the Subjective mind mean to you?

A mighty power resides within you that can give you anything you want. What does the author call it? What would you like to call it?

Mind Connection

The subjective mind is amenable to the objective mind. It carries out to a complete and perfect conclusion of your earnest desires. This is why it's important to train your objective mind on the things and conditions you desire.

Once you have trained your objective mind to focus on your earnest desires, a perfect connection is formed and communicated to the subjective mind that will unfold to your objective mind the method of accomplishment.

The subjective and objective mind are intertwined. How do they relate to each other?

It Works | Workbook

THE PLAN

If you go to work on your goals, your goals will go to work on you. If you go to work on your plan, your plan will go to work on you. Whatever good things we build end up building us.

JIM ROHN

The Plan

- **Write** down in order of importance the things and conditions you really want.

- **Write** down the things you really want in detail.

- **Change** the list daily, adding or taking away from it.

If your desires change, how often should you change your list?

If your desire seems unattainable, should you write it down or not?

Rules of Accomplishment

- **Read** the list three times a day.

- **Think** of what you want as often as possible.

- **Keep** your plans to yourself except to the subjective mind.

The Three Parts (I)

The plan serves three purposes.

First, writing down all the things and conditions you really want gives you a new layer of clarity. You can only know what you want by writing it down and visualizing it.

In each cloud, write down the list of things and conditions you desire.

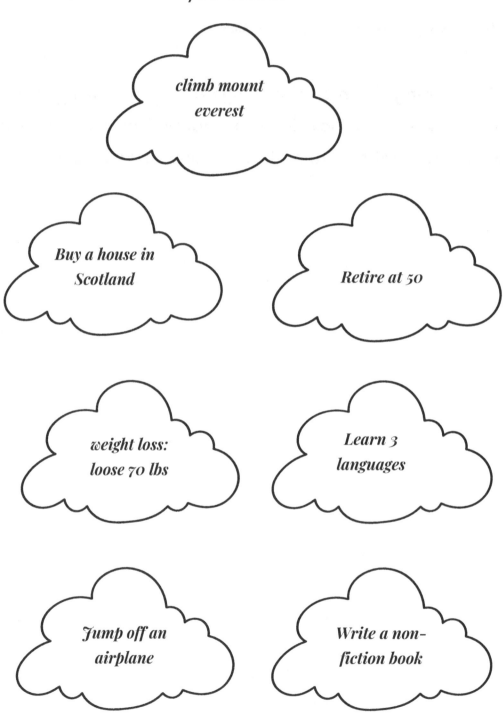

climb mount everest

Buy a house in Scotland

Retire at 50

weight loss: loose 70 lbs

Learn 3 languages

Jump off an airplane

Write a non-fiction book

In each cloud, write down the list of things and conditions you desire.

In each cloud, write down the list of things and conditions you desire.

The Three Parts (II)

Secondly, as you continue to visualize what you have written down, a pattern will emerge. You will notice that some of the things you thought were earnest desires are mere wishes. Now, you will be able to separate the *mere wishes* from *earnest desires*.

You will also be able to group them by **priority**.

As your condition changes within and without, your desires will also change.

List one way or sign that shows that you are making progress with your list?

Is removing from your list a sure sign that you are making progress?

For this exercise, separate your wishes from your earnest desire.

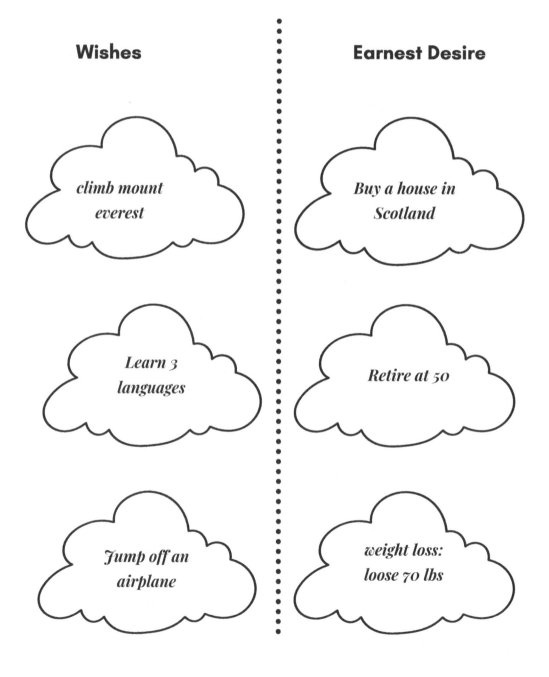

Wishes

Earnest Desire

climb mount everest

Buy a house in Scotland

Learn 3 languages

Retire at 50

Jump off an airplane

weight loss: loose 70 lbs

In this exercise, separate your wishes from your earnest desire.

Wishes   **Earnest Desire**

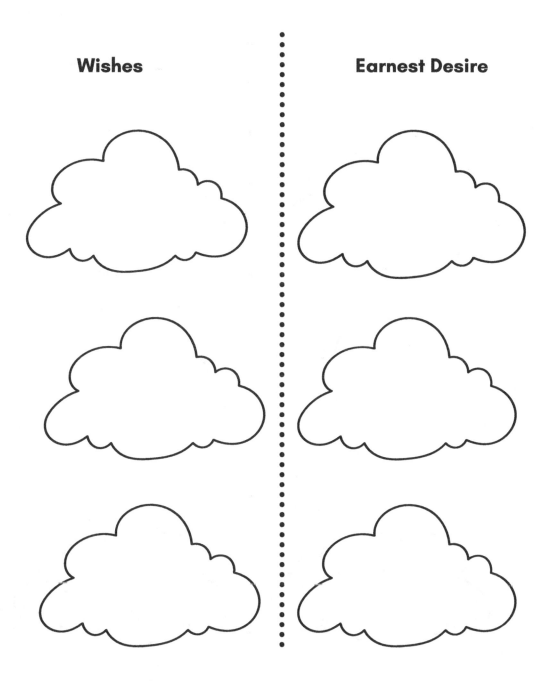

In this exercise, seperate your wishes from your earnest desire.

Wishes   **Earnest Desire**

For this exercise, list your earnest desires by priority.

Earnest Desire

1 *weight loss: loose 70 lbs*

2 *Buy a house in Scotland*

3 *Retire at 50*

4

5

6

For this exercise, list your earnest desires by priority.

Earnest Desire

For this exercise, list your earnest desires by priority.

Earnest Desire

For this exercise, list your earnest desires by priority.

① *weight loss: loose 70 lbs*

② *Buy a house in Scotland*

③ *Retire at 50*

○

○

○

○

○

○

○

○

For this exercise, list your earnest desires by priority.

○ _____

○ _____

○ _____

○ _____

○ _____

○ _____

○ _____

○ _____

○ _____

○ _____

○ _____

The Three Parts (III)

Finally, writing down your earnest desires in detail trains the mind to see them in detail. If you don't know where you are going (what you want), you might end up someplace else (something different).

Detailed visualization is the compass to your destination. In essence, if your objective mind is a house, you are cleaning, re-organizing, and putting your home in order.

Once you know the things you truly desire, reading the list three times a day and constantly thinking about it forms a perfect connection with your subjective mind (omnipotent power) that will unfold to your objective mind the method of accomplishment.

What are the three rules of accomplishment?

For this exercise, list each earnest desire in detail. You should list a minimum of 15.

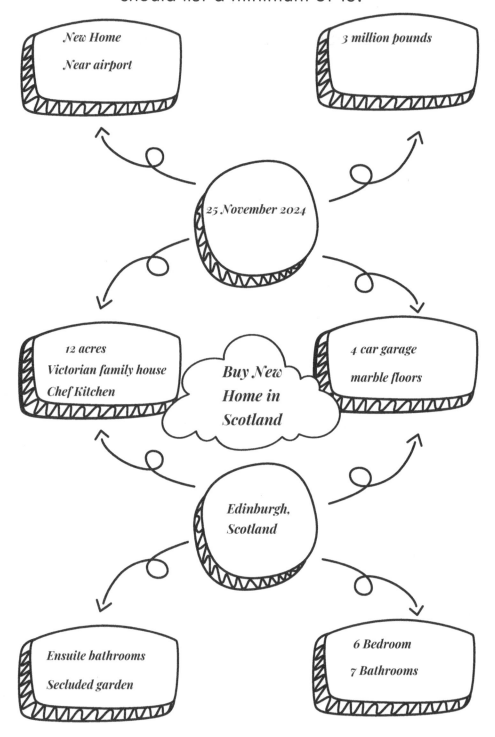

New Home
Near airport

3 million pounds

25 November 2024

12 acres
Victorian family house
Chef Kitchen

Buy New Home in Scotland

4 car garage
marble floors

Edinburgh, Scotland

Ensuite bathrooms
Secluded garden

6 Bedroom
7 Bathrooms

For this exercise, list each earnest desire in detail. You should list a minimum of 15.

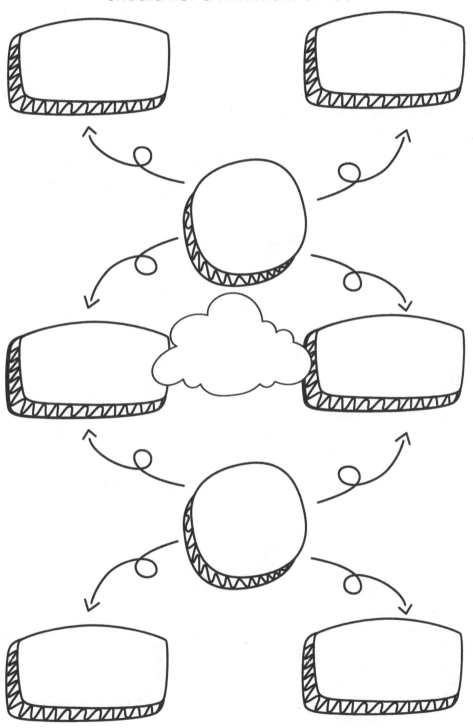

For this exercise, list each earnest desire in detail. You should list a minimum of 15.

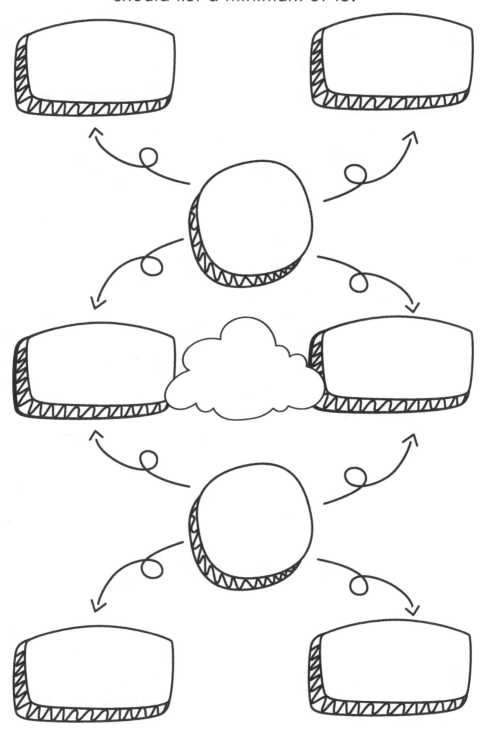

List each item on your list in details.

Review/update		Due Date/
New House in Scotland		*25 November 2024*
New Home	3 million pounds	6 Bedroom
12 acres	Edinburgh, Scotland	7 Bathrooms
Near airport	Victorian family house	Guest house
4 car garage	marble floors	Ensuite bathrooms
Gated entrance	Chef Kitchen	Secluded garden

Keep writing in details

Review/update	Due Date/

It Works | Workbook

DOUBT

Worry, doubt, fear, and despair are the enemies which slowly bring us down to the ground and turn us to dust before we die

ANONYMOUS

Doubt

We all experience some form of doubt in our lives. Doubts come about as a result of different factors. It can come from past experiences, uncertainties, relatives, and friends. Discouragement and doubts are poisons. They kill off earnest desires.

When doubt presents itself to discourage you, you must cut it off from its root. You can accomplish this by:

- Thinking about your plans (visualization or positive affirmation)

- Re-reading your plans.

- Do not tell anyone about it.

The idea is to keep our earnest desires planted firmly in the objective mind so that it continues to maintain a perfect connection with the subjective mind.

If you become skeptical or have doubts about achieving your desires, what is the next thing you should do?

It Works | Workbook

GRATITUDE

If you want to turn your life around, try thankfulness. It will change your life mightily.

GERALD GOOD

Gratitude

Gratitude is being aware of and thankful for the good things that happen in life. In all things, we must show gratitude.

Gratitude is twofold—appreciation and affirmation of goodness. We show appreciation by affirming the goodness, gifts, and benefits we have received. And that the things we have received have been freely given to us.

Give thanks and credit to your subjective mind, the omnipotent power within you, when one of your earnest desires is accomplished.

As you continue to show gratitude, more accomplishments will follow.

What are you grateful for today?

Are they things you accomplished in your past that you failed to show gratitude for? Please list at least five of them and complete your accomplishments with gratitude.

What do you gain by giving thanks and asserting credit to your omnipotent power?

It Works | Workbook

Conclusion

To change your condition and acquire desirable possession, all it requires is earnest effort. Follow the plan and achieve your dreams. It Works.

Trust yourself. Create the kind of self that you will be happy to live with all your life. Make the most of yourself by fanning the tiny, inner sparks of possibility into flames of achievement.

GOLDA MEIR

WorkSheet #1

After reading IT WORKS, answer the following questions below as best as you can. If you find it difficult answering some of the questions, go back and reread the book or the chapter. It's important that you have a full understanding of the key concepts.

People are born under a lucky star that makes them fortunate in life.

☐ Yes   ☐ No   ☐ don't know

The objective mind is the omnipotent power

☐ Yes   ☐ No   ☐ don't know

Training your objective mind is the first step in getting what you want.

☐ Yes   ☐ No   ☐ don't know

Most wishes are simply vocal expressions.

☐ Yes   ☐ No   ☐ don't know

You should read the list of what you want two times a day.

☐ Yes   ☐ No   ☐ don't know

WorkSheet #2

When new desires arise, do not write them on your list.

☐ Yes   ☐ No   ☐ don't know

Nothing can prevent you from getting what you earnestly want.

☐ Yes   ☐ No   ☐ don't know

To realize your desires, you must know positively and in details of what you want.

☐ Yes   ☐ No   ☐ don't know

By given thanks to your omnipotent power, you gain assurance and more accomplishment.

☐ Yes   ☐ No   ☐ don't know

John wants a sport car. He should write down the make, kind, style, price, color and other details of the car

☐ Yes   ☐ No   ☐ don't know

John does not need to write down the date he wants it.

☐ Yes   ☐ No   ☐ don't know

It Works | Workbook

In each cloud, write down the list of things and conditions you desire.

In this exercise, seperate your wishes from your earnest desire.

Wishes

Earnest Desire

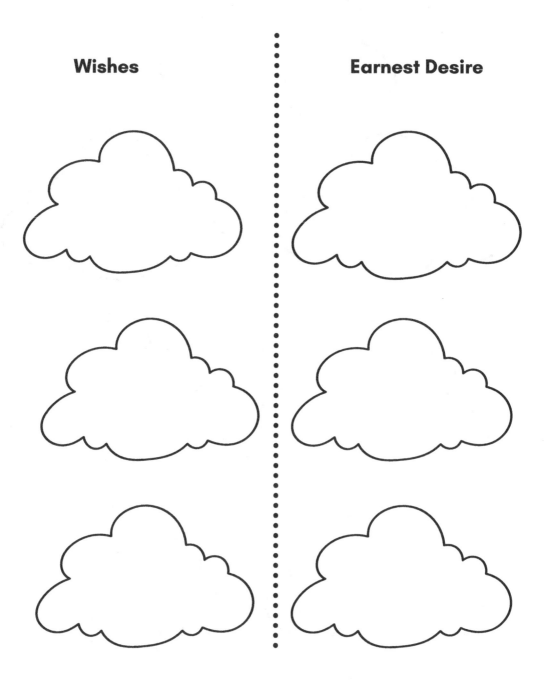

For this exercise, list your earnest desires by priority.

Earnest Desire

For this exercise, list your earnest desires by priority.

○ _____

○ _____

○ _____

○ _____

○ _____

○ _____

○ _____

○ _____

○ _____

○ _____

○ _____

Revise your list in order of importance including when you want it.

☐ _____

_____
Due Date

☐ _____

_____
Due Date

☐ _____

_____
Due Date

☐ _____

_____
Due Date

☐ _____

_____
Due Date

☐ _____

_____
Due Date

☐ _____

_____
Due Date

☐ _____

_____
Due Date

☐ _____

_____
Due Date

☐ _____

_____
Due Date

☐ _____

_____
Due Date

For this exercise, list each earnest desire in detail. You should list a minimum of 15.

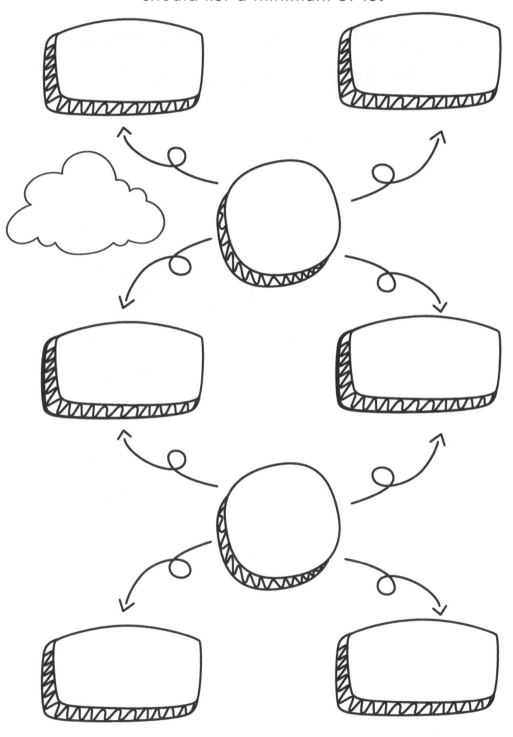

List each item on your list in details.

Review/update   *Due Date/*

Review/update   *Due Date/*

Companion Books

IF YOU KNOW WHAT YOU WANT YOU CAN HAVE IT

IT

WORKS

THE FAMOUS LITTLE RED BOOK THAT MAKES YOUR DREAM COME TRUE

R H JARETT

THE PLAN

WRITE

IT

DOWN

IT WORKS

GREENFIELD BOOKS

Made in United States
Cleveland, OH
14 February 2025

14345321R00052